21st CENTURY LIVES
MOTORSPORTS CHAMPIONS

Paul Mason

WAYLAND

First published in 2007 by Wayland

© Copyright 2007 Wayland

Wayland
338 Euston Road
London NW1 3BH

Wayland Australia
Level 17/207 Kent Street
Sydney NSW 2000

Editor: Dereen Taylor
Designer: Fiona Grant
Design: Peter Bailey for Proof Books
Cover Design: Hodder Children's Books

British Library Cataloguing in Publication Data
 Mason, Paul, 1967-
   Motorsports Champions. - (21st Century Lives)
   1. Automobile racing drivers - Juvenile literature
   2. Motorcyclists - Juvenile literature 3. Motorcycle racing
   - Juvenile literature
   I. Title
   796.7'2'0922

ISBN-978 0 7502 5241 6

Cover: Valentino Rossi.
AFP/GettyImages: 8, 14; ToniAlbir/epa/Corbis: front cover and 18, 19; Steve Boyle/Newsport/Corbis: 17; Manuel Bruque/epa/Corbis: 6; Don Emmert/AFP/Getty Images: 21; Eric Gaillard/Reuters/Corbis: 15; Getty Images: 11; Rainer Jensen/epa/Corbis: 5; Michael Kim/Corbis: 13; Bryn Lennon/Getty Images: 1, 20; Geoff Miller/Reuters/Corbis: 12; Martin Philbey/epa/Corbis: 7; Red Bull Air Race World Series: 10; Schlegelmilch/Corbis: 4; Giampiero Sposito/Reuters/Corbis: 9; Tim Tadder/Corbis: 16.
Every attempt has been made to clear copyright. Should there be any inadvertent omission please apply to the publisher for rectification.

Printed in China

Wayland is a division of Hachette Children's Books, an Hachette Livre UK company.

Contents

Fernando Alonso
Formula 1 driver

Fernando Alonso celebrates winning the Formula 1 World Championship for the first time, after coming third in the Brazilian Grand Prix.

"My parents are responsible for the two things I like doing most – driving and magic tricks. They bought me my first go-kart and a magician's kit."

Fernando Alonso.

Name: Fernando Alonso (born Fernando Alonso Diaz)

Nickname: Magic. He gets his nickname from his skill at card games, rather than his driving!

Sport: Formula 1 racing

Date and place of birth: 29 July 1981, Oviedo, Spain

Background: Fernando won the Formula 1 World Championship in 2005 and 2006, at times seeming unbeatable. He is one of the best racing drivers ever.

Major achievements:
1993-1996: Spanish Junior Karting Champion
1996: World Junior Karting Champion
1999: Euro-Open Champion in his first season racing single-seat cars (six wins, nine pole positions)
Formula 1 career:
2001: 10th at German Grand Prix
2002: Renault test driver
2003: 6th in championship
2004: 4th in championship
2005 and 2006: Winner of championship

You might not know: Fernando's favourite band is the Red Hot Chili Peppers.

Become a pro: Fernando is famous for his calmness, even when he is under a lot of pressure. He says, "I have always been very calm on the outside… For me, tomorrow will be another day whether I finish first or last. I have to do [my best] and I cannot ask any more from myself."

Alonso floors it and leads the pack at the start of the 2006 Monaco Grand Prix.

Fernando started driving at the age of three. His father had built a kart for Fernando's sister, Lorena. Lorena did not like driving the kart – so Fernando inherited it! His feet did not reach the control pedals, so they had to be adapted. But once Fernando could drive, his father began to think that Fernando could one day be a great racing driver.

Driving and racing the kart began to take up more and more of Fernando's time. Fortunately, he was doing well at school, so his mother said it was okay to go to races every weekend! As well as racing in the Spanish kart championships, Fernando worked as a mechanic for younger drivers. This meant he could earn a little extra money to help the family's finances.

By 1998, Fernando had earned a chance to drive a car instead of a kart. It was the first time he had driven anything with gears. Even so, he was soon winning races, and it was not long before he was given a chance to try a Formula 1 car.

Fernando first drove in Formula 1 for the Minardi team. The Minardi car was not fast enough to win races, but his driving attracted the attention of Renault. Fernando was a test driver for Renault in 2002, then raced for them in 2003. A month after his 22nd birthday, he won the Hungarian Grand Prix – the youngest driver ever to win a GP race.

Fernando was even more successful in 2005 and 2006. In 2005, he won seven out of 19 races, came second in five, and finished third in three. Fernando became the youngest driver ever to become world champion, at 24 years and 59 days old.

In 2006, Fernando again won seven races, and came second in another seven. He was world champion once more. On the back of his success McLaren secured Fernando for the 2007 season. Most experts expect that it won't be long before he wins a third world championship.

> "A will to win is what Fernando has always carried inside him. Even though you tell him to go slowly, he does not take any notice. If he… sees an opportunity to go faster, he does it without a second thought."
>
> José Luis Alonso, Fernando's father.

weblinks

For more information about Fernando Alonso, go to
**www.waylinks.co.uk/
21CentLives/MotorsportsChampions**

Nicky Hayden
MotoGP rider

Nicky Hayden celebrates winning the World Championship at the last MotoGP of the 2006 season at Valencia in Spain.

Name: Nicolas Patrick Hayden

Nickname: The Kentucky Kid

Sport: Motorbike racing

Date and place of birth:
30 July 1981, Kentucky, USA

Background: Nicky is one of the world's best motorbike racers, and the 2006 MotoGP champion. He won the title by beating the rider many people thought of as the world's best, Valentino Rossi. He and Rossi are the only riders to win the 990cc MotoGP Championship.

Major achievements:
1999: American Supersport 600cc Championship; American Dirt Track Rookie (beginner) of the Year
American Superbike Championship: 2000, 2nd; 2001, 3rd; 2002, 1st
MotoGP World Championship: 2003, 5th; 2004, 8th; 2005, 3rd; 2006, 1st

You might not know: Nicky has two brothers, Tommy and Roger, and they once finished in first, second and third position in a race. (He also has two sisters, Jenny and Kathleen).

Become a pro: Nicky's advice to up-and-coming motorbike racers is, "Ride hard and often!"

❝ I do enjoy battling with Valentino [Rossi]. It doesn't get any better than him... it brings out the best in people to be right there and fighting with him. ❞

Nicky talks about his season-long battle with Valentino Rossi in 2006.

Nicky Hayden was so young when he started racing motorbikes that his feet couldn't touch the ground when sitting on the bike! Nicky always had to start at the back, with a grown-up holding his bike upright until the race started.

Nicky's first race was a 'dirt track' race at the age of four. This is a kind of racing that is most popular in the USA. The bikes slide round the short track in a spectacular way. Learning to control a sliding bike was a big help to Nicky later. Today he is famous for being able to slide the back wheel of his powerful MotoGP bike sideways into a corner.

By the time he was 16, Nicky had become a professional racer. A year later, in 1999, Nicky and his older brother battled all season to win the American Supersport 600cc Championship. Nicky eventually came out on top, and became the youngest champion ever.

Nicky spent the next three years trying to win the American Superbike Championship. He placed 2nd and 3rd, then won the title in 2002. Nicky decided it was time to move to the biggest, most closely fought races in the world: MotoGP. He wanted to win the World Championship.

In 2003, Nicky won the MotoGP Rookie of the Year Award, finishing 5th overall. His teammate was Valentino Rossi, who won the title in 2003. Rossi won again in 2004 and 2005, with a new, different team. It seemed unlikely anyone could beat him. But Nicky had other ideas.

The 2006 MotoGP championship was one of the most exciting ever. Nicky took an early lead, but Rossi started to catch up. With two races to go, it was neck-and-neck between them. Then disaster struck for Nicky at the race in Estoril, Portugal. His teammate Dani Pedrosa crashed into him, meaning Nicky didn't finish the race. Rossi came second, and took the lead

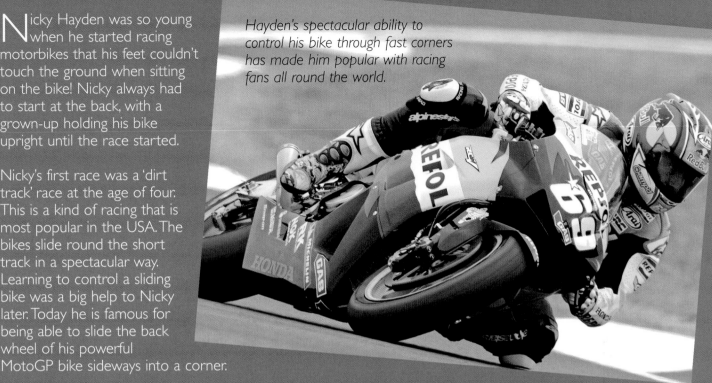

Hayden's spectacular ability to control his bike through fast corners has made him popular with racing fans all round the world.

in the championship. There was just one race to go, and the pressure was on both riders…

In the end, it was Rossi who cracked. He crashed while trying to get to the front, and finished 13th. Nicky finished 3rd, and won the MotoGP title. At last, he was world champion.

"All I can say now is a big 'congratulations' to Nicky because he is a great guy, a great rider and he is the world champion because he has been the best this year. I have known him a long time, I know his family well and even though I am disappointed, I am also very happy for them."

Valentino Rossi after Hayden's victory in the 2006 MotoGP Championship.

weblinks

For more information about Nicky Hayden, go to
www.waylinks.co.uk/ 21CentLives/MotorsportsChampions

Sébastian Loeb
Rally driver

Sébastian Loeb after winning the Monte-Carlo Rally in 2007.

> **To win the title is always a very nice moment for me, my co-driver and all the team. There was a lot of pressure before I won the championship but now it will stay a very good memory and hopefully I will win a few more in the future.**

Sébastian Loeb after winning the World Rally Championship in 2006.

Name: Sébastian Loeb

Sport: Rally driving

Date and place of birth:
26 February 1974, Haguenau, France

Background: Sébastian Loeb is one of the most successful young rally drivers ever. He is often said to be the 'Michael Schumacher of rallying' (Schumacher was world Formula 1 champion seven times).

Major achievements:
1999: Citroen Saxo Trophy Champion
2000: French Gravel Racing Champion
2001: Super-1600 Champion
World Rally Champion: 2004, 2005, 2006
Winner of 28 World Rally Championship events (at the end of 2006)

You might not know: Before he was a rally driver, Sébastian was an electrician. He says that he spent all the money he earned on cars!

Become a pro: Sébastian has a great team around him. Most important is co-driver Daniel Elena, who sits in the passenger seat giving Sébastian directions. Daniel is the most successful co-driver ever in rallying, with over 25 wins.

This jump was a crowd-thriller on the first day of the Rally of Sardinia in 2004.

Rally drivers have to cover all sorts of different surfaces: road, forest track, sand, and even snow and ice. To be fast on all of the different surfaces you have to be a special kind of driver. The best rally driver in recent years – is Sébastian Loeb.

Sébastian's first sports interest was gymnastics, not car racing. His father had been a champion gymnast, and from the age of three Sébastian learned gymnastics too. He was four times Champion of Alsace in France. Eventually, though, the lure of racing became too great and Sébastian gave up gymnastics.

Sébastian began to race mini-moto motorbikes. However, he really wanted to race cars. When he was 21, Sébastian saw an advert for a "Young Rally" competition. He took part that year and the next, and was determined to be fast enough to be a full-time rally driver.

Finally, in 1997, Sébastian got his chance. He was given the chance to race full-time. By the end of the season, he had been voted Best Newcomer by Exhaust magazine. Sébastian spent the next few years driving increasingly more powerful cars, until in 2002 he won his first ever World Rally Championship (WRC) rally in Germany.

2003 was the first year Sébastian took part in all the rallies in the WRC. He won three rallies, and finished the season in 2nd place. In 2004, Sébastian didn't only win the title, he managed six wins, equalling the record for the most wins in a season. In 2005, he broke all records, with ten wins (including six in a row). No one had ever managed to be so far ahead of the competition. People began to say that Sébastian was the best rally driver ever.

In 2006, Sébastian won his third WRC in a row. He couldn't quite match 2005's great performance. This time Sébastian was only able to manage eight wins instead of ten! It was still the second-most victories scored by any WRC driver.

"I think Loeb is probably the greatest rally driver of all time. [He] has shown that he can drive exactly as necessary, on any surface – as fast as the others or just fast enough to let the others make mistakes while he doesn't. In fact, he hardly ever makes mistakes…"

Former rally driver Vic Elford.

weblinks

For more information about Sébastian Loeb, go to
www.waylinks.co.uk/ 21CentLives/MotorsportsChampions

Alejandro Maclean

Air racer

Alejandro Maclean.

Name: Alejandro Maclean

Nickname: The Flying Matador

Sport: Air Racing

Date and place of birth:
6 August 1969, Madrid, Spain

Background: Alejandro Maclean is the youngest pilot in the Red Bull Air Race series. In air races, pilots skilfully fly small planes through a tricky aerial obstacle course in the fastest possible time.

Major achievements:
1998: Winner of the Lithuanian Open Aerobatic Flying Championships
2001: 10th place in the World 'Unlimited' Aerobatic Flying Championships (the top class, for the most experienced pilots)
Twice winner of the European Aerobatic Flying championship
2005: Captain of the Spanish Aerobatic Flying Team

You might not know: Alejandro gets his unusual (for a Spaniard) surname from his grandfather, who was Scottish.

Become a pro: Alejandro is famous for not being put off by dangerous setbacks. In 1992, for example, he broke his back and both legs in a crash. Many people would have been discouraged, but he was soon itching to get back in his race plane!

> ❝ I've come up with a few new tricks that I practised during the winter break. I've been able to get away from big cities when I've had some free time and soaked up some of the peace and quiet out there. Betting on me in the Red Bull Air Race is a good investment. ❞

Alejandro looks forward to a new season of air races.

Maclean flying in the Red Bull Air Race held in Perth, Australia, in 2006. Flying a plane through twisty, tricky air-race courses takes great skill.

When he was a small boy, Alejandro Maclean's bedroom in Spain was filled with models of airplanes. He had made some and collected others. Alejandro dreamed of one day sitting in the cockpit of a real plane and flying it.

The closest Alejandro got to flying a plane for a while was to fly a radio-controlled aircraft. But every summer he worked and saved his money, aiming one day to get airborne. Finally, when he was 18, Alejandro had enough money saved. He bought an ultralight, a small aircraft a little like a hang-glider with a seat and engine.

The ultralight was a good way of learning to fly, as it was slow moving, but easy to take off and land. It introduced Alejandro to the feeling he had dreamed of since he was a small boy: the thrill of flying. Unfortunately, it also introduced him to another experience: crashing!

The small crash Alejandro experienced in his ultralight was not his last. In 1992, he was flying at an air show when the propeller broke off his plane mid-flight. Alejandro survived the crash, but his back was broken in three places, and he broke both legs as well. Even so, he was soon back in the cockpit!

Alejandro's next crash could have been even worse. A new plane he was testing broke up in mid-air and began to plummet to earth. Alejandro quickly ejected from the pilot's seat, but by that time he was only 200 metres from the ground. His parachute only just had time to open and save his life. If he had ejected seconds later, he would probably have been killed.

When Alejandro is not air racing, he's often still up in the sky – in his helicopters or skydiving! His other hobbies include horse riding and waterskiing.

Alejandro still lives in Madrid, where he was born and brought up. He is now married with two children, Alex and Eduardo. If they become pilots as determined and skilled as their father, they may one day be fighting it out to be air race champions.

weblinks ▸

For more information about Alejandro Maclean, go to
www.waylinks.co.uk/ 21CentLives/MotorsportsChampions

Danica Patrick
IndyCar driver

Danica Patrick at the Indianapolis 500 in 2005, when she was the only female racer.

Name: Danica Sue Patrick

Sport: Motor racing

Date and place of birth:
25 March 1982, Wisconsin, USA

Background: Danica is one of the world's best female motor racing drivers. She is the leading female IndyCar racer, and the only woman ever to lead the famous Indy 500 race.

Major achievements:
1994 and 1996: Won US National Points Championship in kart racing
2000: 2nd place at the Formula Ford Festival in the UK, the best finish ever by a US driver
2003: First woman ever to finish in the top three in a Toyota Atlantic Championship race
2004: First woman ever to qualify fastest for a race in the Toyota Atlantic Championship
2005: Races in IndyCar for the first time: finishes Rookie (beginner) of the Year

You might not know: Danica's favourite car is, "Anything fast and black!". She has a pet miniature schnauzer dog, called Billy.

Become a pro: Danica is very competitive once she gets behind the wheel of her racing car! She says about the other drivers, "I need to beat them, belittle them and make them feel small. Trying to run them off the road at 170 mph isn't sweet and kind."

❝I just didn't want to get left out. I still don't. ❞

Danica explaining how she came to be so successful in a sport dominated by men.

Danica Patrick speeds past during the St. Petersburg IndyCar race, which takes place partly on public roads.

Danica Patrick is the most famous female racing driver in the world. Her biggest achievement so far is leading the Indy 500, the only woman ever to have led this race. Considering that there are rarely any women in the race at all, this is an amazing achievement. But Danica has never been scared of being the only female in a race – if she was, she would have given up racing a long time ago.

Danica first started racing in karts when she was just ten years old. She was lapped (overtaken by the leaders) six times in her first race, but she wasn't put off. She carried on taking part in races, and when the points from all the races that season were added up, Danica came second!

Just two years later, in 1994, Danica won her first national points championship. She was still only 12 years old. She carried on racing in karts – she was still too young to drive a car! In 1996, Danica won 39 out of 49 races, and a second national points championship.

By 1998, Danica had started racing cars. At the age of just 16, she left home for England, to race in the Formula Vauxhall series. She carried on racing in England and the USA, and in 2000 finished 2nd in the Formula Ford Festival. It was the best ever result by an American driver.

Danica returned to the USA to race for the famous Bobby Rahal racing team. In 2003 and 2004, she drove in the Toyota Atlantic Championship. First, she became the first woman ever to finish in the top three. Then,

there was an even bigger success: Danica became the first woman in the championship's history to qualify fastest.

2005 was Danica's first season in IndyCar, the top class of car racing in the USA. She carried on breaking records. Danica qualified fastest for three races, and led the Indy 500. *USA Today* named her Female Athlete of the Year, and she won the Rookie of the Year award.

2006 was not so successful. Danica's car kept having mechanical problems, and she could only manage two 4th-place finishes. At the end of the season she moved to a new team at Andretti-Green Racing.

"If you want to be the best lawyer, you go to Harvard. If you want to be the best driver, you go to England."

Bev Patrick, Danica's mother, on letting her daughter move to England at 16 years of age.

weblinks

For more information about Danica Patrick, go to **www.waylinks.co.uk/ 21CentLives/MotorsportsChampions**

Stéphane Peterhansel
Desert Racer

Stéphane Peterhansel celebrates his record-breaking ninth overall win, in the 2007 Dakar Rally.

❝ I used to watch the race on the television, and it was my dream then just to take part in it, never mind to win it! ❞

Stéphane Peterhansel speaking about the Dakar Rally.

Name: Stéphane Peterhansel

Sport: Desert racing

Date and place of birth:
6 August 1965, France

Background: Stéphane is the most successful desert racer ever. He has won the Dakar Rally, the world's toughest desert race, both riding a motorbike and driving a car.

Major achievements:
Winner of the Dakar Rally, motorbike category: 1991, 1992, 1993, 1995, 1996, 1998
Winner of the Dakar Rally, overall category (driving a car): 2004, 2005, 2007
World Motorbike Enduro Champion: 1997, 2001
Winner of the Rally of Tunisia and United Arab Emirates Desert Challenge: 2002
Winner of the Rally of Tunisia and Rally of Morocco: 2004

You might not know: When he was 13, Stéphane won the French skateboarding championships.

Become a pro: Stéphane says that having a good mixture of talents has helped to make him such a good desert racer. When someone suggested he might be unbeatable on a motorbike, Stéphane replied, "I don't think I'm always the fastest rider [but] winning the [rally] means having riding [ability], navigation skills, good tactics, stamina and concentration."

The Dakar Rally crosses huge areas of desert. The drivers have to be able to find their way across sand dunes, rocky areas and steep slopes.

Stéphane Peterhansel has won the Dakar Rally an amazing 10 times. The Dakar Rally is said to be the toughest motor race in the world. It is open to cars, motorbikes and trucks. The race crosses 7,000 miles of rocky, thorny, sandy desert in just 18 days. That's almost 400 miles every single day! The racers often find it hard to be sure which way to go, and can find themselves lost in the desert far from help. To make things harder, during the day the air is baking hot, while at night the temperatures can drop below freezing.

Stéphane had always wanted to be an off-road motorbike racer. "My father is a race mechanic and rode trials bikes", he remembers. "I started riding when I was eight years old and entered my first motocross race at 16." Stéphane did well in racing, and his first really big success came when he won the Dakar Rally in 1991, at the age of 26. No one realised it at the time, but it was the start of the biggest Dakar story ever.

Stéphane went on to win the Dakar five more times on a bike, the last time in 1998. Then he made the astounding decision to try to win the race in the car category as well. He would be up against drivers who had spent years learning the skills needed to win the race in a car.

Only one other driver, Hubert Auriol, had previously won the Dakar Rally both on a motorbike and in a car. Auriol had won three times: on a motorbike in 1981 and 1983 and in a car in 1992. Stéphane said, "After winning six times I hold the record for the most wins [Cyril Neveau had previously won five times] so it's time to move over to cars."

Stéphane came 7th in 1999, 2nd in 2000, and won the T1 car class in 2001. He would have to wait until 2004 to win the overall prize in the Dakar Rally, but Stéphane quickly followed up his victory with a second overall win in 2005. In 2006, he just lost to his teammate, Luc Alphand. Even so, few people thought that this amazing racer's winning ways were finished, and he came back to win the race a 10th time in 2007.

"He [Stéphane] is a reference for all of us. He is fast, strong, really hard to beat… I'm very proud of having been fighting with him until almost the end [of the race]."

Luc Alphand, Stéphane's teammate and winner of the Dakar Rally in 2006.

weblinks

For more information about Stéphane Peterhansel, go to
www.waylinks.co.uk/ 21CentLives/MotorsportsChampions

Chad Reed
MS and SX rider

Chad Reed, celebrating yet another supercross victory.

❝It was pretty crazy... setting my sights on America, it seemed like it was pretty close... I knew I could get here or whatever, but I really never realised how far it really was, and really what I was asking myself to do.❞

Chad explains how he felt about moving from Australia to the USA to race.

Name: Chad Reed

Nickname: Skippy (after a kangaroo character in an Australian TV programme) or Superbad (meaning super good)

Sport: Motocross (MX) and Supercross (SX)

Date and place of birth: 15 March 1982, Kurri Kurri, Australia

Background: Chad Reed is one of the world's top motocross and supercross riders. He was winner of the world's toughest supercross title – the AMA Championship – in 2004.

Major achievements:
1999 and 2000: Australian Supercross Champion
2001: 2nd overall, World Supercross Championship
2003: World Supercross Champion
2004: 1st in AMA Supercross series
2005: 2nd AMA Supercross series
2006: 2nd AMA Supercross series

You might not know: Chad loves the beach: his favourite holiday would include wakeboarding (a water sport which involves riding the wake of a speed boat on a single board), fishing and jetskiing.

Become a pro: Chad has always been determined not to be scared of other racers, however famous they are. As he says, "No one is above anyone else. We are all the same. All of us can be beaten. We are all normal human beings. [So my plan is always] to ride my motocross bike real fast and try to beat everyone."

Chad Reed was born in a small settlement in the Australian countryside. He first started riding a motorbike at the age of three-and-a-half, and took part in his first race when he was only four!

As a young boy Chad dreamed of one day racing in the USA. The AMA race series there is the toughest anywhere. Chad used to watch the famous American rider Jeremy McGrath and dream of one day being as good as him.

It wasn't long before Chad started to do well in contests. He won his first Australian age-group title when he was just seven years old. Chad carried on winning as he moved on to bikes with bigger and more powerful engines. In 1999, at just 17, he won the Australian Championship, and in 2000 he followed this up with another victory. It was time to look for new challenges.

Chad headed halfway round the world, to Europe. He did well in the World Championship series there, finishing 2nd in the competition. Success gave Chad a chance to do what he had dreamed of since he was a little boy – race in the USA.

Chad's new team wanted him to show how good he was before he took part in the AMA National Championships. In 2002, Chad raced on a smaller bike than he was used to, in the Eastern Championship. By the end of the year he had won seven out of the eight races. The team offered Chad a chance to ride in the biggest contest, the AMA Nationals, in 2003.

2003 was a big year for Chad. He won the World Supercross title, managing nine race wins. He was so fast at the end of the season that he won the last six races in a row. Chad seemed likely to be even better in 2004, and that was how things worked out.

In 2004, Chad won the AMA Supercross title – the championship that many riders think is the toughest. He won 10 of the 16 rounds, and never finished out of the top three. To celebrate at the last round, he flew 40 members of his family and friends from Australia to Las Vegas, where the race was held. They watched him finish the race a world champion – and it seemed unlikely to be for the last time.

Chad Reed launches a big jump at the 2006 X-Games in Los Angeles, California.

"Chad hounded me out there for a while and I was just sticking to my lines… We got our backs against the wall and I'm going to try and win every race from here on in."

Chad's great rival Ricky Carmichael on racing with him.

weblinks

For more information about Chad Reed, go to
www.waylinks.co.uk/ 21CentLives/MotorsportsChampions

Valentino Rossi
MotoGP rider

Valentino Rossi's fun-loving personality and incredible record have made him the world's best-paid motorbike racer.

Name: Valentino Rossi

Nickname: Valentino has two: Valé and The Doctor. His race leathers have 'THE DOCTOR' written across the back

Sport: Motorbike racing

Date and place of birth: 16 February 1979, Urbino, Italy

Background: Valentino Rossi is generally thought of as the best, most successful motorbike racer riding today. By 2007, he had won the world championship seven times and was said to be the 7th-highest earner in sport, at an estimated $30 million a year.

Major achievements:
1997: World 125cc Champion
1999: World 250cc Champion
2001: World 500cc Champion
2002, 2003, 2004, 2005: World MotoGP Champion

You might not know: When Valentino first rode a 125cc motorbike, he crashed on the first corner. Next time out, he made it round the first corner – but crashed on the second!

Become a pro: Valentino never lets his opponents think they can beat him. Randy Mamola, a former world champion himself, says that, "Valentino breaks other people's spirits by dominating practice and qualifying."

"If you believe you are the best, you can't get better, and I always want to get better."

Valentino explains how he always tries to improve his racing.

Celebrating another Rossi victory, this time at the Catalonia MotoGP race in 2006.

Once in a while, a racer comes along who seems to be unbeatable. Unless something goes wrong – a crash, or their machine breaking down – no one can get past them. In motorbike racing, Valentino Rossi is such a racer.

Valentino's father, Graziano, was also a motorbike racer. Valentino started riding a motorbike when he was just two years old. Graziano remembers that, "Around the age of four or five he was very curious and was surrounded by some great riders, so he'd always ask 2,000 questions to these guys." Sometimes young Rossi asked too many questions, though, and people would disappear if they saw him coming!

Valentino's mother did not want him to ride motorbikes. She thought they were too dangerous. Instead, he began to drive an 80cc kart. By the time

he was five, Valentino had decided the kart was too slow: his father put him in a more powerful 100cc engine instead. Valentino's father always supported him in his racing. A story says that he even tried to forge documents so that Valentino could start kart racing before the 10-years-old age limit!

By the time he was 16, Rossi was a professional rider. He raced in the Italian and European 125cc category, steadily improving his skills and speed. In 1997, Valentino's big breakthrough came, when he won the 125cc world championship. Valentino moved on to bikes with bigger engines, and in 2001 he won the 500cc world championship.

In 2002 and 2003, Valentino again won the world championship, which was now called the MotoGP. By the end of 2003, he wanted a new challenge. Valentino moved from the Honda team to Yamaha. Yamaha bikes had been struggling to make it into the top three in races. Plenty of people thought that Valentino would find it hard to win a single race.

Valentino wanted to prove that he wasn't winning because the Honda was the better bike, but because he was the best rider. He was proved right when he won the first race, eight further races, and the world title again. He won again, on the Yamaha, in 2005.

In 2006, Valentino's bike broke down in several races, so he was not able to finish them. In the end he lost his title to Nicky Hayden, but finished the season determined to regain his crown in 2007.

"At this moment he is the first [foremost] sportsman in Italy, and overall I would say he's somewhere between the President and the Pope."

Commentator Guido Meda.

Lewis Hamilton
Formula 1 driver

Lewis Hamilton at the 2007 Goodwood Festival of Speed.

"I'm just having a fantastic day. This is history! "

Lewis Hamilton after winning his first Grand Prix in Montreal, 2007

Name: Lewis Hamilton

Sport: Formula 1 racing

Date and place of birth:
7 January 1985, Tewin, England

Background: Hamilton is the most exciting young racing driver for many years, with the most-successful-ever first season in Formula 1.

Major achievements:
1995–2000: Winner of national and international karting titles, ending as World Number 1 in 2000
2003: Formula Renault UK Champion
2004: Formula 3 Euro races: 15 victories
2005: Formula 3 Euro Champion
2006: GP2 Champion
2007: Grand Prix debut at age 22

You might not know:
Lewis was named after the great U.S. athlete Carl Lewis, winner of nine Olympic Gold medals between 1984 and 1996.

Become a pro: Lewis is famous for his dedication, but he says it's also important to enjoy racing: "If I didn't love it, I'm sure I wouldn't be as good as I am today because I'd have put half the effort in… I think [there are] drivers who just rely on their racing ability and don't do the hard yards. When you're young you don't really understand that philosophy: work hard and see the result."

Hamilton's amazing coolness and speed keep him ahead of his teammate, world champion Fernando Alonso.

In Formula 1, few drivers get a chance to race until their mid-20s. Fewer still ever win a race. At 22, in his first year of racing Formula 1, Lewis Hamilton was already winning races and – amazingly – challenging for the world championship. His rise through motorsport is every young driver's dream.

Lewis began motor racing at the age of six, when his father Anthony bought him a kart. Lewis's talent made people sit up and take notice straight away. The owner of the kart track where Lewis raced introduced him to a reporter one day: "This is Lewis – he's going to be a Formula 1 world champion."

Despite his success at karting, life was not always easy for Lewis. His mum, Carmen, and his dad split up when he was two. Until he was 10 he lived with his mum, then he moved to live with his dad, stepmother and half brother, Nicholas. Lewis is very close to his younger brother, who has cerebral palsy, a disease that affects the way his body works and makes some activities difficult or impossible.

When he was younger, Lewis was bullied at school because of his success at karting. He took up karate as a way of defending himself, and by the time he was 12 Lewis was a black belt. The bullies soon disappeared!

Lewis first met the McLaren Formula 1 team boss Ron Dennis in 1995 at a motorsport awards ceremony. "He looked me square in the face and informed me where he was going in his life," Dennis said later. "He told me how he was going to go about his career." Among Lewis's aims was to one day join the McLaren Formula 1 team.

In 1994, Lewis took the first step towards his dream.

Ron Dennis, who had been watching Lewis's racing career, asked him to join McLaren's Young Driver Support Programme. McLaren have guided Lewis's career ever since, from his karting championships to his start in Formula 1.

Lewis's first season in Formula 1 in 2007 set many records for a 'rookie' (beginner) driver. These included:
• being the first driver to finish in the top three in his first three races.
• becoming the fourth-youngest Grand Prix winner ever.
• being the youngest driver ever to lead the world championship, after his fourth F1 race.

As Martin Whitmarsh, chief executive of the McLaren team, comments, Lewis Hamilton seems sure to go down in history as one of motorsports' champions: "It's pretty clear that Lewis ticks all the necessary boxes... there is no reason why he could not become the greatest driver ever."

"I think Lewis is going to rewrite the [history] book... I believe Lewis will create the benchmark for a whole generation of drivers... Lewis Hamilton can become a role model."

Former champion driver Jackie Stewart

weblinks

For more information about Lewis Hamilton, go to
www.waylinks.co.uk/ 21CentLives/MotorsportsChampions

Luc Alphand

Before becoming a racing driver, Luc Alphand spent 13 years as a World Cup ski racer for the French team. He competed in downhill, the fastest type of ski race. Alphand was Downhill World Cup champion in 1995, 1996 and 1997. In 1997, Alphand also won the Overall Championship. He then retired from competition skiing.

Alphand's love of speed soon found a new outlet, when he began a career as a motor-racing driver. He raced in the 2001 European Le Mans race series, driving sports cars on a track, then the GT sports car race series in 2002. However, Alphand's greatest success came in endurance racing.

In 2005, he finished second in the Dakar Rally, and then in 2006 went one better, winning the race ahead of his legendary teammate Stéphane Peterhansel. As Luc said, there are similarities between skiing and endurance racing: "[In] skiing you also need to read the terrain, like the dunes in the desert. It is similar in some ways. You need to decide when to take risks and when to ease off."

Ricky Carmichael

Ricky Carmichael is the best known – and probably the best – motocross (MX) and supercross (SX) rider of all time. He has won the AMA Motocross Championship a record six times, and has won more than 100 races. Ricky first rode a motorbike when he was three years old, and turned professional when his friends were still finishing school, in 1996. By 2000, Ricky had won the first of his AMA MX championships, which he won again in 2001, 2002, 2003, 2004, 2005 and 2006. In amongst these were two 'perfect' seasons, in which Ricky won every single race, in 2002 and 2004. No other rider has ever managed this.

Ricky also raced in the AMA Supercross series, which he won in 2001, 2002, 2003, 2005 and 2006. Ricky retired at the end of the 2006 season.

Marcus Gronholm

Marcus Gronholm started racing motorbikes, when he entered a motocross (MX) race in 1981. He raced MX for five years, until a knee injury forced him to stop. In 1987 – straight after getting his driver's licence – Marcus entered his first rally race. He raced in selected events for the next 11 years, before being spotted by the Peugeot team in 1998.

Peugeot offered Marcus a chance to race a full World Rally Championship (WRC) season for the first time in 1999 and then again in 2000. He was a brilliant success, winning the WRC title in 2000, as well as four individual rallies in 2002. Marcus went on to win the world title again in 2002. He remains one of the best rally drivers in the world, having finished 3rd in 2005 and 2nd in 2006.

Jutta Kleinschmidt

Jutta Kleinschmidt is famous as the first (and so far, only) woman to win the Dakar Rally, the toughest off-road motor race in the world. Jutta first heard of rallying in 1985, and was fascinated by the idea of the Dakar race. Two years later she followed the rally as a spectator – on a motorbike! It made her determined to take part in the race as a competitor.

In 1992, she had her first success, winning the Ladies Trophy in the Dakar Rally on a motorbike. Shortly afterwards, Jutta switched to car racing.

In 1997, Jutta became the first woman to win a stage of the Dakar Rally. In 1998, Jutta held the overall lead in the rally for three days, proving that she one day might be able to win it. Then, in 2001, Jutta's dream came true: she became the first woman ever to win the Dakar Rally. She remains one of the event's best drivers – male or female.

Michael Schumacher

Michael Schumacher is one of the most successful racing drivers ever. He spent over 10 years at the top of the Formula 1 tree, and won the driver's championship an amazing seven times – more times than any other driver. He is said to have been the first sportsman to earn over a billion dollars in his career.

Michael is best know for three things: 1) his attention to every detail that could help his car go faster, 2) being able to keep up a lightning pace for lap after lap, and 3) his win-at-all-costs driving style. On more than one occasion, crashes with other drivers stopped them from beating Michael, and some experts thought the crashes were deliberate.

Although hard-nosed on the track, Michael is a generous man away from the racing scene. For example, he gave $10,000,000 to help victims of the 2004 Indian Ocean tsunami recover from the disaster. He retired from racing in 2006.

Casey Stoner

Casey Stoner is one of the youngest riders ever to take part in the MotoGP motorbike racing world championship. Casey's family was so keen to help him become a top rider, they moved from Australia to Europe so that he could take part in top-level races!

Casey started racing in MotoGP in 2006, for the LCR Honda team. After a promising start, his season tailed off. However, for the 2007 season, Stoner moved to the Ducati team, whose faster bikes offered him more chance of

victory. He immediately settled into a groove at Ducati. The team was relatively small and close, and was often described as being like a family. This seemed to suit Casey more than racing for the giant Honda organisation. In addition, because this was his second year in MotoGP, Casey knew the race tracks better. He knew where to go fast, and the danger points where too much speed would lead to a crash.

The 2007 season was Casey's best yet, by a mile. He won the season's opening race, in Quatar, where his bike's amazing top speed helped him defeat former world champion Valentino Rossi. In the next race, Casey came fifth. Some people asked, had he won in Quatar only because of his bike's speed? No – Casey went on to win again in Turkey, China, and Catalunya. Then he really proved his skill, in a crucial showdown with Rossi at the British GP.

The race was run in difficult conditions, with heavy rain at the start. The track dried through the race, making the special wet-weather tyres on the bikes difficult to control. These were just the kind of conditions everyone expected Rossi – one of the most skillful riders ever – to win in. But Casey took the lead halfway through the race, and won by a huge gap. Rossi finished a distant 4th, and Casey seemed well on his way to his first MotoGP title.

Index

21st Century Lives

Contents of more books in the series:

WAYLAND